The Truth About Winning!

Gate 4: Orientation to Tennis Reality

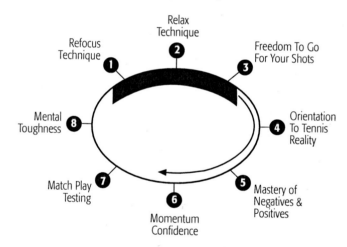

Tom Veneziano

The Truth About Winning — 3rd Edition

Copyright © 2006, 2001 Tom Veneziano Enterprises

All rights reserved. Printed in the United States of America. No part of this book may be used, reproduced or transmitted in any manner whatsoever without written permission from the author except in the case of brief quotations embodied in critical reviews. For more information, contact Tom Veneziano, 10855 Meadowglen Lane #1022, Houston, TX 77042.

Editor and Designer: Mary A. Sicard

ISBN 0-9716203-9-3

Dedication

To my mother and father Virginia and Philip Veneziano, whose gentle, but firm guidance gave me the values upon which my life was built. I love them both.

To R.B. Thieme Jr., whose unique ability as a principle-oriented teacher has profoundly impacted my life. I am eternally grateful.

And to all of my tennis students. You have taught me well.

Contents

Introduction **11**

Level 1: Basic **15**
    Your Perception of Negatives and Positives 15
    Is This Positive Thinking? 15
    Lack of Critical Information 17
    Do Negatives Threaten You? 18
    Negatives Should Not Discourage 19
    The Choice Is Yours 20
    Is Competition Bad? 21
    Taking Responsibility 21
    The Mental Two-Step 22
    Review 23

Level 2: Intermediate **25**
    A Technique to Help You Stay Positive 25
    Learning From The Best 27
    The Mental Toughness Sphere 28
    The Refocus Technique 29
    You Need A Recovery Technique 31
    The Intermediate and Advanced Refocus Technique 32
    Application of the Refocus Technique 33
    Learning The Easy Way 34
    Review 34

Level 3: Advanced **35**
    Evaluating Negatives and Positives 35
    All Positives Are Not Positive 36
    All Negatives Are Not Negative 36
    An Emotional Problem 36
    Do Not Emote. Evaluate. 37

Contents

    Put Emotions Aside 37
    Think Like a Pro 39
    Review 40

Level 4: Professional 41
    Negatives and Positives Applied to Winning 41
    Develop Long-Term Thinking 41
    Tilting the Odds in Your Favor 42
    The Key to Developing Mental Toughness 43
    A Dose of Reality 45
    Hitting Winners: A Result, Not A Cause 45
    A Pro Figures It Out 46
    A New Mind-Set 47
    Tournament Tough 50
    Will This Be You? 51
    Tennis Warriors Are Mentally Ready 54
    Force Your Opponent to Concentrate 56
    Bringing Both Mind-Sets Together 57
    The View of Champions 59
    Isolated Situations vs. The Big Picture 60
    Environmental Stories 61
    A Different Way of Thinking 62
    Review 63

Level 5: The Tennis Warrior 65
    Unexplored Territory 65
    One Step Beyond 66
    Keen Insight 67
    A Thinking Paradox 68
    A Formula for Success 69
    Are You Getting It? 70
    Are You a Pseudo-Perfectionist? 71
    Characteristics of Tennis Warriors 72
    Champions Think Differently 73

Contents

Level Summaries 75
Level 1: Your Perception of Negatives and Positives 75
Level 2: A Technique to Help You Stay Positive 76
Level 3: Evaluating Negatives and Positives 76
Level 4: Negatives and Positives Applied to Winning 77
Level 5: Unexplored Territory 78

Chart of The Tennis Warrior System 81

Books and Tapes by Tom Veneziano 82

Introduction

Welcome to "The Truth About Winning." I have been a tennis pro for over 25 years and have taught many players to win. I work extensively with the mind and developed The Tennis Warrior System. The Tennis Warrior System is a system of thinking that makes it easier to understand tennis concepts and to develop mental toughness.

My books and tapes are interrelated. The more you read and listen to them, the better you'll understand the concepts I present, the better you'll see the big picture, and the better you'll play.

They will help you develop or improve your critical thinking skills so you can use the Mental Toughness Sphere—a tool that helps players develop mental toughness. It has eight gates or mental skills. (This book is part of the Mental Toughness Sphere's "Gate 4: Orientation to Tennis Reality." See the chart on Page 80.)

You'll be able to select the correct weapon from an arsenal of information in your mind. And when you do, you'll become a true Tennis Warrior.

You will not be intimidated by the ups and downs of a match. You'll become self-sufficient and learn to play in a more instinctive and automatic way.

In short, you will become mentally tough and win more.

Here are a few things you'll learn:

- How to stay positive in the face of negatives.
- What negative thinking really is.
- Two mind-sets that increase your chance of winning.

You'll advance through five levels. Each level builds upon the previous level and reveals the truth about winning. The levels are:

Level 1: Basic
Your perception of negatives and positives

Level 2: Intermediate
A technique for staying positive

Level 3: Advanced
A master principle for evaluating negatives and positives

Level 4: Professional
Negatives and positives applied to winning

Level 5: The Tennis Warrior
Unexplored territory

The Tennis Warrior is a thinker who has learned the art of being mentally tough. The Tennis Warrior accomplishes this by accumulating valuable information that can be used at the proper time.

The Tennis Warrior's mental toughness is not reserved only for playing pros. It is for players of every level. You can learn to think correctly whether you're a beginner or a championship player.

Mental toughness is in the mind. Therefore, Tennis Warriors seek information that builds their minds so they can instinctively make the correct mental decisions in a competitive event.

Anyone can learn to be a Tennis Warrior. However, it may be necessary to let go of some incorrect ideas that are not rooted in proven success principles. These principles are often misunderstood for two reasons.

The first reason is that when success is finally achieved, it always appears complicated. What is achieved may be complicated, but that does not mean the process of reaching that achievement is complicated.

Here's a phrase I have my students use:

Do the simple right. Then, do the simple better. Then, simply be the best at doing the simple.

The pros do the simple so well that we think it is complicated, but we're confusing the outcome with the process.

The second reason success principles are often misunderstood is that everyone desires success, but few want to do what is necessary to succeed. They desperately search for shortcuts and abandon the true pathways to success. The outcome is pseudo-success. This type of success is not founded on proven success principles, and these individuals fall apart when the pressure is on.

Hundreds of books promise shortcuts to success. Here's the title of a tennis book on the market that says it all: "Learn to be an 'A' Player in a Weekend."

Do you think many tennis players would buy that book?

True success principles are often talked about, but rarely applied. If you're interested in shortcuts and aren't interested in the process of success, my book is not for you.

However, if you want to learn the truth about winning, my book is definitely for you. You will learn principles that can be applied in any sport or business or in your life.

I have been involved in sports as a player or coach for most of my life, and believe the athletic arena is simply a microcosm of life. In sports, as in life, you face negative and positive situations that require skillful mental maneuvering and problem-solving capabilities. You contend with self-doubt, discouragement and despair as well as conviction, encouragement and inspiration. Your confidence, character and self-esteem are challenged.

How your mind handles challenges in the athletic arena is similar to how your mind handles challenges in business and life. If you justify and rationalize your mistakes and failures in sports, you will do the same in life. If you blame everyone and everything for your failures in sports, you will do the same in life. If you have many successes in sports and become carried away with yourself, you will do the same in life.

On the other hand, if you handle failures and successes correctly in the athletic arena, you will do the same in life.

The way you think in sports is the same way you think in life, and the way you think in life is the same way you think in sports.

It is *your* thinking, and you bring your thinking to whatever arena you may be in, whether it's sports, business or life.

One always influences the other.

Even though this is a book about tennis, what you will learn reaches beyond the athletic arena into the core of your thinking. I hope you are prepared. If you aren't, when you're finished reading this book, you will be.

Now, on with the truth about winning.

Level 1: Basic

Your Perception of Negatives and Positives

One of the most important aspects of winning is learning how to lose correctly. If this seems like a paradox, it was intended to be.

To learn how to win, you must learn how to lose correctly.

That's a powerful phrase. Does it make you say, "I thought winning was about thinking positive thoughts, not negative. The only thing positive about that phrase is the word 'correctly' and what you want me to do correctly is lose?"

Be positive, act positive, think positive and win. Doesn't that sound like something from one of those motivational seminars? It sounds great, so why not—no matter what—think positive? Don't let any negatives enter your mind. In fact, let's go to the courts where Miss Patty Positive is playing a match.

Is This Positive Thinking?

Little Patty Positive is in the middle of a point. She is playing well. All of a sudden, she nets an easy shot. Patty is an

Level 1: Your Perception of Negatives

excellent proponent of positive thinking and does not recognize the miss. She stays positive and moves on. She doesn't let any negatives enter her mind.

This same miss happens three more times, and all three times, Patty stays positive. She doesn't allow the negative of all the misses to enter her mind. The match ends. Patty Positive loses, but Patty pats herself on the back for staying positive the whole match. Even her friends compliment her on her ability to ignore the misses and stay positive.

Although this sounds like the ideal situation, within it lies a subtle pitfall. The pitfall relates to the misconception and misinformation that most people have about positive thinking.

Most people think (either consciously or subconsciously) that to stay positive, they should not think of any negatives. They think negatives are bad and keep them out of their minds.

This simply is not true.

If this is contrary to what you believe, please keep reading. My goal is to give you the truth about winning and that truth starts here.

When players have trouble winning and come to me for advice, I tell them I want them to lose. They just about go ballistic. This is the opposite of what they expect to hear and probably the opposite of what you expected to hear. I explain that I do not want them to lose on purpose. I want them to practice having the correct mental attitude toward mistakes and losses.

Until you accomplish this, forget everything else. No strokes, strategy or magical pieces of technical information will help you.

You must give yourself the freedom to go for your shots, and if you miss, accept it.

This attitude frees you to keep fighting, to keep challenging yourself and to keep taking risks. You do not want your failures or mistakes to be so important in your mind that they stop you from performing. Practicing the correct mental attitude during mistakes and losses is a high priority.

The logic behind this is simple. All players have strengths and weaknesses, and you have to practice your weaknesses to improve. Do you know anyone who has trouble handling wins? (I doubt it.) Do you know anyone who has trouble handling losses, mistakes or failures? (I'm sure you do.)

You must practice your weaknesses to improve. If your thinking is right, do not worry about the results. Eventually, you will win. That's the easy part. The difficult part is learning how to think correctly.

Lack of Critical Information

Misconceptions are created by the lack of certain critical information in sports, business and life. This lack of information often leads us to develop incorrect preconceived ideas.

In the case of negatives, that critical information is the ability to distinguish between acknowledging a negative that affects your mental attitude and acknowledging a negative that does not.

Recognizing a negative is not negative thinking. Negative thinking is when you allow the negative to affect your mental attitude. One mental attitude leads to a distorted view (the negatives divorce you from reality), and the other mental attitude recognizes a negative for what it is—a negative.

Recognizing a negative for what it is (a negative) is perfectly healthy and can produce an undistorted view and a correct orientation to reality. It does not have to affect your mental attitude.

Let's go back to Patty Positive. Patty didn't recognize any negatives and, as a result, she didn't realize the shot she missed time and time again was a low-percentage shot. (A low-percentage shot is one you successfully execute only a small percentage of the time.) Patty was preoccupied with avoiding a negative and didn't analyze what was happening correctly. She should not have attempted a low-percentage shot.

Her fear of negatives distorted her perception of what happened. This distorted perception easily could have been the reason she lost. It was not the mistakes, the failures or the negatives that were the problem. It was her reaction to them.

If negatives, mistakes or failures drastically affect your overall mental attitude, you have a problem. It is perfectly all right to recognize and analyze negatives when they occur. Negatives give you valuable feedback, allowing you to make corrections so the same mistake doesn't happen again.

It takes longer to reach your goals if you don't assess negatives correctly. This is true for sports, business or any situation that calls for a positive mental attitude. Negatives are not your enemy—unless, of course, you are threatened by them.

Do Negatives Threaten You?

Negatives may threaten you, because you have been brainwashed to believe they are the bad guys and recognizing them means you are a negative person.

This is simply not true. Negatives are not the problem.

Negatives may also threaten you, because you have incorrectly connected negatives and mistakes to who and what you are as a person. You may think mistakes and losses aren't just a part of an athletic event; they are an all-consuming part of how you personally feel about yourself.

Somehow, either consciously or subconsciously, you think you are a bad person if you perform poorly and you are a good person if you perform well. Unknowingly, you made a quantum leap from being a good tennis player to being a good person.

Level 1: Your Perception of Negatives

Let me set the record straight. There is no connection between the ability or talent you possess as a tennis player and the quality and character of the person you are—whether you're the best or the worst player in the world.

Do negatives, mistakes or failures discourage you or challenge you? Can you consistently deal with negatives without becoming disillusioned or discouraged? My guess is that you let negatives discourage you. Most people deny failures or rationalize their mistakes to maintain confidence. They have not yet learned how to handle negatives, mistakes and failures and remain confident. This book will teach you how.

The first thing you must do is stop thinking that acknowledging negatives, mistakes or failures is a sign of weakness. Recognizing negatives does not mean you are a negative person. The ability to think in terms of negatives and stay confident is a sign of strength, not weakness.

If this confuses you, hang in there. You'll learn something in the next few paragraphs that will make your game more fun. At the same time, it will make you mentally tougher at anything you do in life.

Negatives Should Not Discourage

One of the principles the Tennis Warrior masters is:

Mentally tough people can think negative thoughts without becoming discouraged.

I love that phrase. The secret that unlocks the whole realm of confidence is: "without becoming discouraged." In other words, mentally tough people can think of negatives as much as they wish. They just don't become discouraged. (And if they do, they bounce back quickly.)

This implies the negative itself is not the problem. There must be thinking going on in the mentally tough person's mind that is different from the thinking going on in the mind of the person who is not mentally tough. After all, both have to face negatives.

The obvious difference is that mentally tough people do not let negatives affect their overall mental attitude. They view negatives and failures for what they are: valuable feedback necessary to reach their goals. They know negatives, mistakes and failures will always be there. This is orientation to reality.

You will still make mistakes even if you are No. 1 in the world. Therefore, it only makes sense to change the way you perceive and are affected by negatives, mistakes and failures.

The Choice Is Yours

You can choose to be discouraged by negatives or you can choose to be challenged by negatives. It's up to you.

Do you know what that means? It means—and get ready for some cold-hearted truth—negatives, mistakes and failures are not the problem.

You are.

The way you perceive and deal with negatives is of paramount importance when you're learning the truth about winning.

Negatives are not the enemy. You are.

When I point the finger at you, remember you purchased a book titled, "The Truth About Winning." That is what I am giving you. And, when I say you are the problem, I do not exclude myself. I had to learn to perceive and deal with negatives correctly. We are in this together, so welcome aboard.

Is Competition Bad?

The idea that competition is bad is seeping into our society in sports, in business and in all areas of life. The proponents of this philosophy say, in essence, that competition brings out the worst in us, causing us to become—well, let's just say—not very congenial. People engage in arguments and fights. They cheat. Sabotage their opponents. Do whatever it takes to win.

This is fuel for the advocates who contend competition makes us behave unseemly. Also, they contend if one person wins, someone loses and that is not nice. This is unequal and therefore, unfair. The person who loses feels bad about himself and that could undermine his self-esteem.

This is a blatant, idiotic, goofball, nonsensical absurdity. America's greatness was brought about by hard work, individualism and self-reliance combined with cooperation and—yes—competition.

The inevitable result is the development of character and self-esteem. Anti-competition advocates should read this next sentence carefully. You acquire self-esteem and character by changing the way you think inside, not by changing the outside circumstances that affect your thinking.

Competition is not at fault.

Taking Responsibility

Why do I bring this up? Because I love America. It is the greatest country on earth, and to see it undermined by people expecting equal opportunity to ensure equal outcome disturbs me. Just because I have equal opportunity does not mean the results of what I do will be the same for everyone else. Some succeed and some fail. Some are better and some are worse. Some win and some lose.

There is no equality of outcome in sports or life.

Another reason I bring this up is because the way some people view competition (as the villain) is the same way people view negatives. It sounds like this: The negatives, mistakes and failures are the culprits. They make me feel down on myself. It is not my fault.

Interesting, isn't it? Few people take responsibility for their decisions. There is such great emphasis on blaming problems on external causes that new theories and philosophies help us rationalize why negatives, mistakes and failures are not our fault.

With these blame-someone-else philosophies, you can blame your bad decisions, mistakes and failures on the environment, the competition or your partner.

As a result, taking responsibility for your own decisions is becoming obsolete. Yet, like it or not, taking responsibility for your own decisions is the solution, especially when dealing with negatives.

You choose how you perceive negatives and how they affect your mental attitude. Tennis Warriors or mentally tough individuals confront these issues and decide to control negatives. Have you?

The Mental Two-Step

You must make two decisions:

1. To recognize the negative.
2. To let it affect you or not let it affect you.

This is the Mental Two-Step. The first step, recognizing a negative, is not negative thinking. The second step, deciding if you will let it affect you, is the determining factor.

The choice is yours.

Let the negative affect you and you choose a negative mental attitude. Do not let the negative affect you and you choose a positive mental attitude.

You are always two mental steps away from a positive or negative mental attitude.

When you realize that acknowledging negatives is not bad, and that thinking positive does not mean you always have to think positive thoughts, you've made it. You passed Level 1. You are on the way to understanding the truth about winning.

So, before we leave Level 1, remember:

Acknowledging negatives is not negative thinking.

Negative thinking is when you let the negative affect your mental attitude. Mentally tough people think in terms of negatives without becoming discouraged. You must learn to do the same.

Review

- The concept of negative thinking is misunderstood.
- You are not a negative thinker because you recognize negatives.
- Recognizing negatives is not the problem. The problem is letting negatives affect your mental attitude.
- Allowing negatives to affect your mental attitude is wrong. It is negative thinking.
- Recognizing negatives that do not affect your mental attitude is right. It is positive thinking.
- Whether or not negatives affect your mental attitude is totally up to you.

Level 2: Intermediate

A Technique to Help You Stay Positive

It's time for a test. Here's the scenario:

Player A and Player B are in a three out of five set match. The score is two sets to one. Player A is winning. The score is 6–6 in the fourth set. They play a tiebreaker that ends with an unbelievable 18–16 victory for Player B.

Player A had seven match point opportunities, but could not put Player B away. This means the score is tied at two sets apiece. A fifth set will have to be played to decide the winner.

Player A, who was up two sets to one with seven match points in the fourth set, feels as if he should have won the match. Before starting the fifth set, he thinks, "I am going to lose."

Here's the test:

Is Player A, the player who thought he was going to lose, a positive thinker who is mentally tough, or a negative thinker who isn't mentally tough?

If you said he isn't mentally tough, you are wrong. Remember? Acknowledging a negative does not mean you are a negative thinker. What Player A does next will determine if he is mentally tough or not.

If he allows his loss to affect his mental attitude, he is thinking negatively. If he does not, he is thinking positively.

Level 2: A Technique To Help You Stay Positive

Remember, you are always two mental steps away from a negative mental attitude or two mental steps away from a positive mental attitude. Recognizing negatives does not mean you are a negative person. The deciding factor is the second step: how it affects your attitude.

You're probably thinking: If someone thinks they're going to lose, there is no way they could be mentally tough.

How did I know that is what you're thinking? Because I ran this scenario by a few friends. Their response was: There is no way that person is mentally tough.

I told myself I had to come up with something pretty strong to make them believers. Well, being the little finagler that I am, I already had something that would shock them. It will shock you, too.

The match scenario I explained is true. It really happened. It happened between two of the best tennis players in the world. It was the extraordinary 1980 Wimbledon final between Bjorn Borg and John McEnroe.

Borg won in the fifth set after losing the fourth set tiebreaker in a devastating 16–18 loss, where he had seven match points to put McEnroe away.

In an interview after the match, Borg was asked what he was thinking after he lost seven match points and then lost the fourth set. Borg said, "I thought I was going to lose."

Let me explain why Borg acknowledged this. Actually, it is not that difficult if you understand the Mental Two-Step. Borg acknowledged the first step. When you are two sets to one up and lose seven match points in the fourth to someone as great as McEnroe and then lose the set, you realize there is a tremendous momentum shift in favor of your opponent.

This happens a lot in sports. (Momentum is important.) Borg was merely orienting to tennis reality. Recognizing a negative for what it is—feedback to help him assess the situation correctly. He knew McEnroe would have momentum and would be motivated playing the fifth set. This easily could have made for a blow out in the fifth if Borg had let this affect him.

So, when he said, "I thought I was going to lose," he was simply evaluating the situation. It was what he said next that determined his attitude. Borg said, "I realized my only chance was to forget what happened and play the fifth set like it was the only set, and do the best I could."

Obviously, his best was good enough, because he won. Notice, the first step did not determine his attitude. Just because he thought he was going to lose did not make him a negative person. It is the second step that was important: he stayed positive.

Learning From The Best

If someone as mentally tough as Borg can think he is going to lose, then mental toughness or staying positive does not mean you always have to think positive thoughts. You can relax and accept your negatives and failures as a reality. Once you do, you can quickly start looking for the solution.

Look how fast Borg went from, "I thought I was going to lose," to the correct attitude for the fifth set. The mental adjustment that Borg made from the first step to the second step did not come from out of nowhere. It was the result of experiencing a similar situation over and over and over again. Sometimes succeeding. Sometimes failing. But always practicing the correct thinking.

You can do the same.

The next time you're thinking negative thoughts, do not think they are unique to you. Everyone, including the pros, has negative thoughts. The key is to push the negative aside, practice staying positive and determine what should be done.

Do not let the negative affect your attitude.

I have a technique that helps you stay positive. It's part of the Mental Toughness Sphere.

Level 2: A Technique To Help You Stay Positive

The Mental Toughness Sphere

The Mental Toughness Sphere is a tool that helps players develop mental toughness. It has eight gates or mental skills:

Gate 1: The Refocus Technique
Gate 2: The Relax Technique
Gate 3: Freedom To Go For Your Shots
Gate 4: Orientation to Tennis Reality
Gate 5: Mastery of Negatives and Positives
Gate 6: Momentum Confidence
Gate 7: Match Play Testing
Gate 8: Mental Toughness

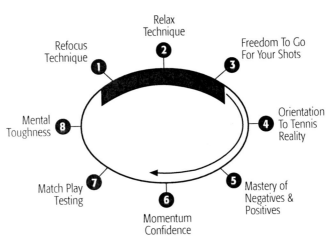

Mental Toughness Sphere

All gates interact with each other. You work your way from "Gate 1: The Refocus Technique" to "Gate 8: Mental Toughness" by accumulating and applying correct tennis knowledge incorporated in the sphere.

You can also tap other sources of knowledge, including coaching, trial and error, books, tapes or a combination of all four. Because trial and error takes time, you can shorten the learning curve tremendously through good coaching, books or tapes.

The Mental Toughness Sphere incorporates an abundance of mental techniques and tennis knowledge. This book is part of the Mental Toughness Sphere's "Gate 4: Orientation to Tennis Reality."

If you have trouble pushing negative thoughts aside, the "Gate 1: Refocus Technique" will help you stay positive.

The Refocus Technique

The Refocus Technique, along with Gates 2 and 3, is the foundation for the other five gates that complete the Sphere. It is one of the mental tools you can use to keep you inside the Mental Toughness Sphere. It helps you stay objective in the face of adversity, and is designed to shift you from thinking with your emotions to thinking with your mind.

When emotion dictates, you have trouble dealing with mistakes and negatives. It controls your thinking and convinces you that you are bad, the experience is horrible or the situation is unfair. Perhaps a little self-pity slips in.

The trick is to get yourself out of the control of your emotion and under the control of your mind. Your thinking must control your emotion rather than your emotion controlling your thinking.

Use this phrase when you are in trouble:

The next shot is more important than the last mistake.

Say it over and over again.
"The next shot is more important than the last mistake."
"The next shot is more important than the last mistake."
Repeat this phrase between points until you can shift from thinking with your emotion to thinking with your mind when

Level 2: A Technique To Help You Stay Positive

you're having trouble with negatives, mistakes or failures. Do not serve or return serve until you have cleared your mind of the last mistake.

The conflict between emotion and the mind is ongoing. You must learn to recognize the difference between your emotion controlling your mind and your mind controlling your emotion.

Obviously, there is nothing wrong with having emotions, but you have a problem if you let emotion control you. If your emotion controls your thinking in an athletic event, making the decisions necessary to win consistently will be tough.

You must control your incorrect emotional response to negatives, mistakes and failures and your incorrect response to success to develop mental toughness.

Your mind must control your emotions. That is why it is called mental toughness. Study the chart below. Notice how the emotion completely reverses the correct mental responses.

Correct Mental Response	Incorrect Emotional Response
You tell yourself the next shot is more important than the last mistake.	You tell yourself the last mistake is more important than the next shot.
You stay objective, and don't take mistakes personally.	You slip into subjectivity, and take mistakes personally.
You do not react to negatives and positives. You treat them in a similar manner.	You react to negatives and positives with wide emotional swings that alternate between self-pity and self-adulation.
You realize your game (whether it's good or bad) is not a reflection of your character.	You perceive your game (whether it's good or bad) as a reflection of your character.

When the last negative, mistake or failure becomes more important in your mind than the next shot, your emotion is controlling you. You must use the Refocus Technique and take back control with your mentality.

The Refocus Technique is a powerful weapon if you learn to use it. As with any technique in tennis, you will be able to use this weapon only through practice and repetition.

You may want to write, "The next shot is more important than the last mistake," on a small piece of paper and stick it on your racket as a reminder, or make up your own phrase. I teach a 15-year-old boy named David who has his own phrases. We work on the Refocus Technique and he is learning extremely fast to forget his mistakes and move on. Two of the phrases he uses to shift from a negative to a positive are:

- I have missed before. It is no big deal.
- To be good, I have to make mistakes.

These phrases pop into his mind when he starts having trouble. They are both excellent. It has been amazing to watch David take control of his thinking. My hat is off to him.

You Need A Recovery Technique

In every failure, in every area of life, you need a recovery technique. If you do not have some way of forgetting your negatives, mistakes and failures, you might as well forget about learning the truth about winning. You just won't get it. You will always be hung up on the short-term solution and miss the big picture.

The Refocus Technique can be a powerful tool to help you stay positive and focused. It can help you move on to thinking about what you should do next and stop you from dwelling on your mistakes and failures. Your emotion dwells in the past. Your mind, with the correct information, keeps you in the present, thinking about what you should do next.

If you practice the Refocus Technique enough, it can ac-

Level 2: A Technique To Help You Stay Positive

tually be fun. You will be one of the few who understand how to deal with negatives correctly. This gives you an edge in any field. You can and must learn how to stay positive in the face of negatives.

The Intermediate and Advanced Refocus Technique

The Refocus Technique has a basic, intermediate and advanced level. Your goal is to reach the advanced level where reminders such as "The next shot is more important than the last mistake," are not as necessary.

How do you accomplish this? It's simple: practice. The more you use the Refocus Technique, the less time it takes to recover from mistakes.

At first, recovering and moving on from your mistakes or a series of mistakes may take you a minute or two (or, in some cases, 10 -15 minutes or more). As you continue applying the Refocus Technique, you slowly reduce your recovery time until one day you mentally shift from a negative to a positive automatically.

At the intermediate level, you still use a phrase to help you recover, but you're moving on quickly.

At the advanced level, moving on from your failures becomes a way of thinking. You no longer need to use a phrase to remind you.

Practicing the Refocus Technique consistently trains and conditions your mind to make a quick and automatic mental shift from a negative to a positive without hesitation.

The majority of good pros recover instantly. They have mastered the Refocus Technique so well they no longer separate their negatives, mistakes and failures from their successes or wins.

Success and failure are part of the process of winning. The great past heavyweight boxing champion Jack Dempsey once said, "Success and failure are the same. The only difference is success gets up and keeps moving."

You must learn to think the same way.

Apply the Refocus Technique consistently until your negatives, mistakes and failures aren't an issue.

Application of the Refocus Technique

Let me apply the Refocus Technique to the Borg vs. McEnroe match. In the fourth set, Borg had an opportunity to put McEnroe away but didn't capitalize on it. This led him to believe McEnroe would have a tremendous boost, and, as a result, Borg knew it could cost him the match.

At this point, Borg thought he was going to lose. This was step one of the Mental Two-Step, acknowledging the negative. Then, he used his version of the Refocus Technique, quickly going from step one to step two: the solution.

He knew he had to forget about the last set and play the next set as best as he could. He did not focus on the past (incorrect emotional response). Instead, Borg focused on the present (correct mental response). In essence, he realized the next set was more important than the last loss.

Borg was capable of going from step one to step two extremely fast because of experience. When I say he used his version of the Refocus Technique, I mean whatever went on in his mind to make him forget about the past and focus on the solution. At Borg's level, the experience of being in similar situations over and over again made this second nature. Switching from step one to step two was automatic. The good pros realize this is what it takes to win consistently.

You must be able to switch gears quickly after negatives. This is what mental toughness is all about. I cannot emphasis enough the importance of the Refocus Technique.

One of the first things you learn when you drive a car with

Level 2: A Technique To Help You Stay Positive

a stick shift is how to neutralize the engine by pushing in the clutch. By doing this, you disengage the engine so you can shift to another gear.

This is identical to the Refocus Technique. By bringing your mind back to neutral, you can then shift to another mental gear. Using the clutch to bring the engine to neutral keeps the car running smoothly just like the Refocus Technique helps you play more smoothly, even in rough terrain.

Learning The Easy Way

You can learn this lesson from hard knocks or you can apply the information in this book and shorten your learning curve tremendously. Use the Refocus Technique as much as possible during tough times and it eventually becomes automatic.

Review

- You are always two mental steps away from a positive or negative mental attitude.
- Use the Refocus Technique when you're having trouble dealing with negatives and mistakes. Think: "The next shot is more important than the last mistake."

Level 3: Advanced

Evaluating Negatives and Positives

You may want to evaluate what went wrong or what went right after a match is over or after you use the Refocus Technique. You need the master principle to do this correctly. That principle is:

All negatives are not negative and all positives are not positive.

How's that for confusion? I never said thinking was going to be easy. Thomas Edison said it best: "There is no expediency man will not go to avoid thinking."

The master principle is extremely important in any situation where the correct mental attitude is essential for optimum performance—which is just about all the time.

All negatives are not negative and all positives are not positive.

Just because things work out well does not mean you have done something correctly, and just because things work out poorly does not mean you have done something incorrectly. Most people pair winning with doing something right and losing with doing something wrong.

All Positives Are Not Positive

For instance, you are playing tennis and you're up at the net. You take a low ball and go for a winner. The winner lands in for a great shot. You congratulate yourself and move on. You won; therefore, you did something right.

It never dawns on you the winner could have been a low-percentage shot, which makes you lose more points in the long run, thus making it the wrong time to hit it.

In other words, the shot you hit worked out well, but the thinking was incorrect.

All positives are not positive.

All Negatives Are Not Negative

You are presented with a high, short ball at the net. It has "winner" written all over it. You see the open court and go for it. Unfortunately, you miss, and in your mind, you think you did something wrong. It doesn't occur to you that the shot you tried to make was the right shot at the right time. It was what you were supposed to do. The shot you hit did not work out, but the thinking was correct.

All negatives are not negative.

An Emotional Problem

I must caution you at this point. Your emotions will have a very difficult time accepting this. Emotion will keep telling you, "Who cares if I was thinking correctly? I lost the point."

As I said earlier, most people pair winning with right and losing with wrong. Whether the thinking was correct is irrelevant. Well, it's time to change—at least if you want to learn the truth about winning.

Level 3: Evaluating Negatives and Positives

It is imperative that you understand when you're thinking correctly and when you're thinking incorrectly, regardless of whether you win or lose.

To accomplish this, you must put aside your emotion.

Do Not Emote. Evaluate.

I have a friend named Sam Lacava from New Jersey. Sam and I attended the same high school and college. We both played tennis, table tennis, racketball and other racket sports.

Sam has exceptional hand-eye coordination. We both became tennis pros. Sam still teaches some tennis, but ventured into the business world and is very successful. We discussed various problems when he began his own business. A variety of subjects came up in our conversations: handling negatives, evaluating situations properly, keeping your emotion in check when making decisions, etc.

After tossing ideas around for a while, I came up with a phrase to simplify everything:

Do not emote. Evaluate.

Sam called me a month later. "Tom, it really works," he said. He used that phrase each time a problem came up. He's worked himself out of impossible situations many times, because he instinctively shuts off his emotion and evaluates the problem objectively.

Put Emotions Aside

Why is this important? Because you need to put aside your emotions to evaluate correctly. You must evaluate objectively, without that false reality your emotion tells you is real.

Level 3: Evaluating Negatives and Positives

Let's go back to the high ball you missed when you were up at the net. Remember? The thinking was correct, but you missed the shot.

How would your emotion react? What kind of analysis would your emotion come up with? Do you think your emotion would be happy about the situation?

Your emotion does not care if the thinking is right or wrong. You miss. You lose the point. And you mistakenly think, "I lost the point. I did something wrong. If I win a point, I've done something right." That is the way your emotion reacts.

Emotions think short-term, not long-term.

Your emotions have no concept of long-term success principles. (That is why we have coaches—to teach us these principles.) If you have a situation where you win a point, but have no business hitting that shot, your emotion deceives you into believing this is the way to win. After all, even though it was a low-percentage shot, you won the point.

The problem is, you will incorrectly evaluate what it takes to win if you are winning but thinking incorrectly. It catches up with you eventually and you won't know what to do.

You must start evaluating without emotion. Just because you lost the point does not mean you were thinking wrong. If you had a high, short ball, and it was time to go for it, do it. If you miss, forget it and move on. (Use the Refocus Technique: "The next shot is more important than the last mistake.")

You were playing it right. Your thinking was correct. You were not indecisive when it was time to go for the winner. If you keep practicing, eventually you will make the shots.

Make this a habit and guess what you'll do when you find yourself under pressure? You will do what Tennis Warriors do: you will go for it, because that's what you've trained yourself to do.

This is the reason why the top touring pros play so well under pressure. They mentally train themselves for years to think objectively, evaluate realistically, and come to a correct conclusion.

Think Like a Pro

Just like the pros, you'll have many opportunities to practice thinking right when hitting a winner. Just like the pros, you'll have many opportunities to miss. And just like the pros, if your thinking is correct, you'll forget the miss and move on.

Remember, you are training yourself to develop the correct mental attitude. When it's time to go for it, go for it! This is long-term thinking and your emotion has nothing to do with it.

If you go for the wrong shot and win the point, learn to recognize your thinking was incorrect and do not make a habit of it. Recognize when you have incorrectly won so you won't be fooled into believing that is the way to win.

In the long run, correct thinking pays huge dividends. You are developing the correct mental attitude, and the correct mental attitude is essential when learning the truth about winning.

Evaluate on the basis of whether your thinking was right or wrong, not on the basis of if you won or lost the point.

Now, that doesn't seem too difficult, does it? Well, your emotion, the great deceiver, will be ever present to distort your thinking if given the opportunity. It is up to you. Use the Refocus Technique when necessary, and do not emote. Evaluate. You will be on your way to controlling your emotions instead of your emotions controlling you.

I am not saying emotion is bad. Emotion is fine as long as it responds to the mental. Incorrect emotion can be a source of tremendous energy, but it is usually short lived and does not provide any long-term consistency, which is necessary for competition.

Level 3: Evaluating Negatives and Positives

Review

- All negatives are not negative.
- All positives are not positive.
- Do not emote. Evaluate.

Level 4: Professional

Negatives and Positives Applied to Winning

Congratulations. You've reached Level 4. Now, you need a goal. Then, you'll need the necessary information to accomplish that goal. Combine these and you'll have a plan you can use every time you play, or—with a little modification—you'll have a plan to use for business, living or anything else.

Let's get right to it. Your goal is to:

Create and maintain an environment that gives your opponent the greatest potential to crack under pressure.

Everything you do and think is subordinate to that goal, and you must handle negatives correctly to accomplish this. This is why Levels 1, 2 and 3 are important. If your mind constantly becomes discouraged by your mistakes and failures, the only environment you'll create is one in which you—not your opponent—will be prone to crack.

Develop Long-Term Thinking

Your emotion dictates when mistakes and failures come into play. Your emotion thinks short-term, not long-term. This is a major problem, because you need to think long-term, not short-term, to create and maintain the correct environment.

It is crucial that you develop a long-term focus. An excellent example of this is rearing children. You create the proper environment for them day after day, week after week, month after month. You don't do this for just one or two days and expect good results.

The same is true for winning. You must create and maintain the correct environment day after day, week after week, month after month.

Creating and maintaining an environment means you think long-term, not short-term. So what do I mean by creating and maintaining an environment "that gives your opponent the greatest potential to crack under pressure?"

Tilting the Odds in Your Favor

Giving your opponent the greatest potential to crack under pressure means you maximize your physical and mental skills to the point where your opponent can no longer stay with you.

In other words, your opponent becomes more prone to make physical and mental mistakes. You must tilt the odds in your favor to accomplish this.

In tennis, the three areas you can maximize to create an environment that tilts the odds in your favor are:

1. Physical Fitness
   If you are fit and never run out of steam, that is one plus in your favor for creating the proper environment for winning.

2. Stroke Production
   The more consistent your strokes are, the more balls your opponent has to hit.

3. Mental
You've heard it before: "Their strokes are terrible, but they beat all the good players." The mental part of your game can offset the other two areas when applied correctly.

The Key to Developing Mental Toughness

Here is a definition of mental toughness:

Mental toughness is the accumulation of valuable information used at the proper time.

Most people think mental toughness is never giving up, determination or perseverance. Although these traits describe a mentally tough person, a Tennis Warrior accumulates a lot of information and applies it at the proper time.

Tennis Warriors develop a mental toughness arsenal in their minds and instinctively select the correct information for different situations. This helps them to persevere, to never give up and to stay determined.

You need to begin accumulating information so that it's available to you at the proper time. This book is loaded with information that will help.

Do not treat what you are about to learn lightly. It takes players years and years of match play coupled with trial and error to develop these mind-sets or ways of thinking. Even then, many do not figure it out. You have an opportunity to learn it now and cut years off of your learning time.

You must adjust your thinking in two areas to maximize the mental and create the proper environment:

- You do not win by trying to win.
- Tennis repeats itself, so lighten up.

These mind-sets help you orient to tennis reality and give you the final pieces of information that teach you the truth about winning.

Let's examine the first mind-set:

You do not win by trying to win.

You really don't. In sports, people think you win by doing something spectacular or exciting or by hitting home runs or winners. They try to win by winning. This is a mind-set.

In business, a mind-set might be placing a glossy ad in a magazine a few times, and hoping it makes your business a success. When it does not work, you never advertise again.

Don't get me wrong. There is nothing wrong with hitting a home run or winner, placing a glossy ad or looking for a big score. The problem is developing a mind-set that thinks (consciously or subconsciously) this is the way to win, this is the way to succeed. As a result, you make decisions based on that mind-set.

For instance, you may think hitting winners is the way to win in tennis, so the decisions you make during the warm up and the match are subordinate to that thinking. During the warm up, you hit the ball too hard or try to hit winners, never giving yourself or your opponent a chance to warm up properly. (For more information on warming up correctly, listen to my tape, "Before-Match Pointers.")

During the match, you try to do too much with the ball every time it comes to you. You are going to win the point *now*. In your mind, that is the way to win, and you make decisions based on the wrong mind-set. Your unforced errors go up, and you lose points needlessly. (Unforced errors are errors you make that are self-created.) You are overanxious even when you simply try to keep the ball in play. If the ball comes back two or three times and you have not put it away, you think you've done something wrong. So, you try to hit a winner on the next shot—even if it's the wrong time.

This is human nature. We are all susceptible to it. I'm not telling you to never hit winners or to hit the ball right back to your opponent every time. You can make your opponent move all over the court without constantly thinking you have to hit a winner. When the opportunity presents itself, then go for it.

Consistency first. Winners second.

A Dose of Reality

Tom Landry, who was the great head coach of the Dallas Cowboys football team, said, "Coaching is getting people to do what they do not want to do in order to achieve what they want to achieve."

I have been coaching for over 25 years and, believe me, this could not be truer. People want to achieve, but all too often, they do not want to do what it takes.

The "You do not win by trying to win" mind-set is just such a case. No matter how many ways I say it, it seems to be human nature to think the opposite.

You are wrong if you think you have to do something dynamic, something spectacular or something exciting to win. Sorry for being so blunt, but this is a tough mind-set for people to break. I have tried to be more diplomatic in the past, but it just does not work. So, for the sake of communicating the principle and getting the truth across, I have reduced it to its simplest form: You are wrong.

Hitting Winners: A Result, Not A Cause

Hitting winners and home runs or doing something spectacular are results, not causes. You do not win tennis matches by hitting winners. You do not win baseball games by hitting

Level 4: Negatives and Positives Applied to Winning

home runs. You do not build a business running one or two glossy ads, and you do not make a lot of money by looking for one big score.

What percentage of all the hits in baseball is home runs? It doesn't take a statistical genius to figure out it's a very small percentage. As far as tennis is concerned, winners probably average 10 to 20 percent on a professional level. That's all.

Are you asking, "If I don't win by trying to win, exactly what do I do?" (Good question. I thought you would never ask.) You learn to develop an environment that makes all of these things happen naturally. Winners, home runs, big scores and the spectacular happen as a result of creating the correct environment.

They are not causes.

You must stop thinking winners win matches. "But, wait a minute," you say. "The other day I was up at the net, and I took a low ball and knocked it off for an angle winner. It was spectacular. And I won the game."

This is precisely why the concept of creating an environment for winning is so difficult to understand. Remember the master principle? All positives are not positives.

Yes, you won the point, and yes, it was a great shot, but it was an exception, not the rule. If you allow yourself to evaluate honestly, you would admit you could only make that shot one out of five times.

Do not build a long-term game plan around exceptions.

A Pro Figures It Out

Here's how a former Top 10 pro created the proper environment. The pro was Gene Mayer, and he explained in a tennis magazine article how he thought he had to hit winners, hit lines and do spectacular things to beat the top players when he first broke into the pros. He finally figured it out. Instead of going for the lines, he hit the ball a few feet inside the lines. He made his opponents hit more tennis balls by doing this and found better opportunities to go for winners.

He discovered he did not have to do something spectacular to win points. He reasoned that even though these guys were pros, he still had to make them hit the ball to make errors.

He was right. With the other mind-set, he was trying to hit too many spectacular shots and, as a result, he was the one making the errors. (Keep in mind he was a touring pro when he caught on.)

He felt that understanding the principle of creating the proper environment and applying it was one of the main reasons he did so well. Gene learned to create and maintain an environment that gave his opponent the greatest potential to crack under pressure. The winners he hit came as a result of creating that environment.

You must do the same.

A New Mind-Set

Stop trying to win by trying to win. It's the difference between making it happen and letting it happen.

Your greatest competitors let it happen. If they see opportunities to make it happen while they are letting it happen, they seize them. Tennis Warriors realize that letting it happen means following the correct principles consistently and letting those principles work. They are not always trying to hit winners. Instead, they play steadily, moving the ball around and looking for openings. This creates and maintains an environment that gives their opponents the greatest potential to crack under pressure.

Everything you do mentally is subordinate to that goal. Notice, I did not say create and maintain an environment that

Level 4: Negatives and Positives Applied to Winning

gives *you* the greatest potential to crack under pressure. This is what most players do unknowingly. They constantly try to hit winners or to do something exciting. Just creating and sustaining the proper environment is exciting enough.

You do not achieve this goal immediately. The process is long-term. You set up the correct environment to succeed. If, while doing this, you have opportunities to hit winners, that's fine. You have put winners and winning in their proper perspective. They are results, not causes.

Can this be applied to life? You bet. Here is a true story. Many years ago, I had some serious financial problems. I looked for quick ways to make money to get back on track. Every one of those quick fixes ended in disaster. I was simply looking for the big score. I should have known better. I eventually woke up and realized I had to plod my way back, and that I'd better start now.

Here's what I did: I automatically deducted $25 per month out of my account and put it in a mutual fund. This doesn't sound like much, but the important thing was to start thinking correctly and create the proper environment.

As the months went by, I increased the amount to $50, $75, $100 and so on. As the fund accrued, other opportunities opened up for me and I slowly recovered. It took time, but I did it. The keys to my financial recovery were thinking correctly and creating the proper environment.

This is exactly what I did in the athletic arena. When I was in trouble, I slowly worked my way back into a match. Of course, life situations can be a lot more serious, but the principle still applies.

The next time you're in a match, stop playing as if every shot has to win the point. Work on creating and maintaining the proper environment. Move the ball around. Use the correct mind-set. And when the opening presents itself, go for the winner.

Create the environment first, and winners and winning will

come as a natural result. You'll discover that most points are won or lost before anyone has an opportunity to hit a winner. You do not have to do spectacular things to win.

Developing and mastering this first mind-set is a big part of the truth about winning. Of course, if you cannot handle your mistakes and failures correctly, and your evaluations are all emotional reactions, trying to adopt this mind-set will be close to impossible. You'll be too busy being flustered to evaluate and follow any kind of long-term plan.

But all that applies to someone else—not you—right? You've mastered the Refocus Technique. You do not emote. You evaluate. And now you won't have any trouble following the correct mind-set, right? (I knew I could count on you.)

The second mind-set necessary to learn the truth about winning is:

Tennis repeats itself, so lighten up.

Combine the "You do not win by trying to win," mind-set with "Tennis repeats itself, so lighten up," mind-set, and I guarantee you are on your way to success. Your percentage of wins will increase dramatically.

What happens on the tennis court repeats itself—just like history. We learn from history that we learn nothing from history. Unfortunately, the same is true for tennis. All too often, we don't learn from events that repeat themselves. Events repeat themselves for you and events repeat themselves for others.

It is not unique to you if you had some bad luck and lost the point. This happens over and over again. You're passed at the net with a blazing shot from your opponent. This is not unique to you. It happens over and over again. You had an easy shot and missed. This is not unique to you. It happens over and over again. You were ahead 5-1 and lost. This is not unique to you. It happens over and over again.

These and many other situations happen over and over and over again. What happens on the tennis court repeats itself. You may be saying, "You're right. All of these things have happened to me. It's horrible. I know I have to correct these problems before I can win, right?"

Wrong. These things happen all of the time, yet champions still win. They miss easy shots and still win. They have bad breaks and still win. They are passed numerous times and still win. They play poorly and still win.

Look at the big picture. Think long-term. Do not isolate these situations. Thinking short-term stops you from seeing the big picture. These situations always occur—whether you win or lose, so you might as well get used to them.

Tournament Tough

Here's an excellent definition of tournament toughness from Carlos Goffi's book, "Tournament Tough."

> Tournament toughness is that mental resilience and flexibility that separates the champions from the pack, allowing them to win against opponents who are technically more skillful and physically more powerful even when they themselves are playing poorly.

Mentally tough competitors do not play perfectly to win. They improvise when confronted with obstacles and adverse situations. Interesting, isn't it? All this time you thought everything had to go just right to win. In fact, if you are like most players, you have a preconceived idea about the way you think you should play. When this doesn't occur, you become frustrated, angry and emotional.

Since tennis, or anything else in life, doesn't happen exactly the way you think it should, you have unrealistic expectations. You spend a lot of time being frustrated. As a result, you lose confidence and start playing tentatively or you just mentally quit.

Will This Be You?

Getting players to part with false expectations can be difficult. After reading this book, you may go out and play, miss an easy shot and immediately you say, "I make that shot all the time. What happened? Why did I miss? I cannot believe how horrible I am playing. I am never going to win."

Voila. You immediately begin playing tentatively. Somehow, your mistakes cannot possibly be the same as the mistakes I have been writing about. The reason you think this way is good old-fashioned rationalization.

You say: "I make that shot all the time. I should not miss."

I say: "It's obvious you don't make that shot all the time because you just missed."

You have unknowingly created two categories of mistakes: mistakes you think are all right to make and mistakes you think are not all right to make. You use the correct thinking on the shots you miss that you think are all right to miss, and incorrect thinking on the shots you miss that you think are not all right to miss.

Do not separate them.

The tennis repeats itself principle applies to both categories of mistakes, from the simple to the complex. The truth is that you are too preoccupied with the problem and you ignore the solution. You are so hung up on your preconceived ideas about the way you expect yourself to play that you're mentally distracted by certain mistakes and never apply the solution.

And the solution is:

Tennis repeats itself, so lighten up.

Level 4: Negatives and Positives Applied to Winning

Your situations and mistakes are no different from anyone else's. You must get over this hurdle to understand the truth about winning. You don't have to play perfectly to win. I am not telling you to like these situations or to never attempt to analyze and make corrections. Obviously, you have to practice and keep improving.

When you're in a match, you'll never reach perfection. You could be No. 1 in the world and you are going to make mistakes. In the long run, your mistakes will not be the deciding factor on whether you win or lose. The deciding factor will be how you choose to deal with your mistakes.

This is also true in life. If you spend all of your time agonizing over past mistakes, you will never achieve success. You must refocus and move on.

To create and maintain the proper environment, you must learn to think correctly in negative situations. You cannot let negatives, mistakes and failures disrupt the environment you are trying to establish. This can be extremely difficult because human nature expects quick, band-aid-type solutions.

Have you noticed how, when a basketball player loses the ball or makes a stupid mistake, he tends to compound the problem by committing a foul right after the mistake? What you've just learned explains why this occurs.

The player wanted a quick, band-aid-type solution to the problem, because he made a mistake. He thinks: If I can quickly get the ball back, I will solve the problem.

As a result, he overplays, commits a foul, compounds the problem, and loses the correct long-term environment. Notice, the problem was not the first mistake he made. The problem was his reaction to the first mistake.

Let me stop right here to help you understand a mental subtlety of this situation. I have been a teacher for most of my life and one of the pitfalls of explaining different mental concepts is this: Everyone says, "Okay, I got it," but they proceed

Level 4: Negatives and Positives Applied to Winning

to the court and think exactly the opposite of what they just said they understood.

There is a difference between intellectual understanding and application understanding. I cannot bring you to the tennis court to watch you play and make sure you have application understanding. However, I can explain what you are thinking and what you will think when you are actually in the same situation yourself by using the basketball example.

This is the best I can do in hopes you'll catch on to intellectual and application understanding and not fall prey to this subtle mental pitfall.

Here is the problem. As you read the basketball example, you thought to yourself: That makes sense. When I make a mistake, don't try to compensate for it by overplaying and making additional mistakes. This destroys the correct long-term environment I am trying to create and maintain. I must forget my negatives, mistakes and failures and move on.

Very good. You've got it. Or do you? Well, right now, you are calm, relaxed and objective. This isn't the mind-set you have after you've made a few mistakes. You must imagine the feelings—the anger, disgust, self-doubt and embarrassment—you experience when you make a mistake or a series of mistakes. Suddenly, you have a different scenario.

When you're on the court and experience these horrible negative feelings, you must make a decision not to react so you can maintain the correct mental environment. It is not easy. You must not give into the emotional thinking that entices you to overplay while trying to correct the mistake you just made. Become familiar with the way you feel when you make a mistake that bothers you the next time you play. Remind yourself that it's at that moment you must make those correct decisions.

It's essential to be aware of how you feel when you experience negative feelings and to understand those feelings. Choosing the correct solution is the first step towards solving the problem of emotional reaction.

Forget the failure and move on—even in the face of negative feelings. This whole scenario explains why players tell me they understand, but then do the opposite.

They do not make the correct application when they are preoccupied with the negatives, mistakes and failures. You must learn to think correctly in negative situations. This separates you from the rest of the pack and allows you to maintain that crucial long-term environment. It is the signature of a Tennis Warrior. You will not believe the difference it makes in your entire mental attitude once you think correctly in negative situations.

Tennis Warriors Are Mentally Ready

Remember, tennis repeats itself. You will make mistakes a certain percentage of time whether or not you like it. It's inevitable. Smart competitors know this and adjust their thinking accordingly. Instead of fighting mistakes, they master them. They formulate a plan to handle them beforehand, because they know these mistakes are going to happen. Tennis Warriors clearly understand that to win consistently, they must learn to control adverse conditions and minimize their affect.

If you know certain mistakes and problems will occur ahead of time, you will not be surprised when they do occur. Tennis Warriors are well aware of this. When opponents blast a shot by them for a winner, they are mentally ready. They know this situation has happened before. When they make a series of mistakes, they are mentally ready. It has happened before.

On a day when they cannot to do anything right, Tennis Warriors are mentally ready. It has happened before. When opponents play perfectly, Tennis Warriors are mentally ready. It has happened before.

Are you mentally ready? What would you do if all of these negatives happened to you? Would you think: I am just not

Level 4: Negatives and Positives Applied to Winning

playing well. Why should I even try? Or: I am playing horribly. That's why I can't win.

Well, you no longer have these excuses. I am telling you now (and have been telling you) that it does not matter. You can win regardless.

Sure, you could play badly and lose, but you can also play badly and win. Tennis Warriors understand the big picture. Knowing these things will occur helps them stay mentally focused when they do occur. Tennis Warriors realize that understanding the big picture and handling negatives correctly are part of the process of winning. They are masters at weathering the storm, minimizing the affect of these situations and turning them into a formidable weapon. Tennis Warriors create and maintain an environment that gives their opponents the greatest potential to crack under pressure, even when they are under pressure.

You must learn to do the same.

Here is a list of negatives that happen a percentage of the time—whether or not you like it. (Do they look familiar?)

- You hit the net cord and the ball falls on your side.

- Your opponent hits the net cord and the ball drops on—yes, you guessed it—your side.

- You make stupid mistakes.

- You make a string of mistakes or play horribly.

- Your opponent plays perfectly.

- You are on the verge of victory, and then lose.

- You miss an easy shot.

- You have bad breaks.

- Your opponent has all the breaks.

- Things you never expected to happen will happen.

This is only a partial list. What you should remember is: tennis repeats itself. These things are always going to occur. To create and maintain an environment that gives your opponent the greatest potential to crack under pressure, you must practice dealing with adversities correctly.

You do this by firmly planting in your mind the fact that tennis repeats itself, so lighten up.

Force Your Opponent to Concentrate

Let me show you a subtle, but important, benefit of thinking this way. If you are thinking correctly when the tough times hit, you will keep fighting. Why will you keep fighting? Because, tennis repeats itself. You knew ahead of time tough times were going to occur. You now realize dealing with them correctly is part of winning. This forces your opponent to concentrate to beat you.

If you are thinking incorrectly, when the tough times hit, your opponent does not have to concentrate to pull off a victory. You are so down on yourself, he or she can relax and still win. It doesn't take a Ph.D. to figure out that if you make your opponent concentrate, he or she has to do something to win.

You have seen this many times while watching the pros. First, one pro is winning. Then, all of the sudden, the other pro is winning, and so on. One gets on a roll. The other hangs in there and forces the opponent to keep concentrating. The pros know mental lapses are inevitably if they force their opponent to keep concentrating. The pro is poised to grab the momentum back when these lapses occur.

If the pro didn't hang in there during the tough times, the opportunity would not have existed. In fact, the match would have been over long ago.

The principle of forcing your opponent to concentrate to beat you is one of the benefits of adopting the "tennis repeats itself" mind-set. And, if that is not enough, here is another benefit.

You relax when you recognize that adversities are not an issue, because you know they can occur. You free yourself to go for your shots, take a few risks, and simply play tennis. You will be the player to emulate.

Bringing Both Mind-Sets Together

Here are the two mind-sets you should master:

1. You don't win by trying to win.
2. Tennis repeats itself, so lighten up.

You must learn to use both of these. They help tilt the odds in your favor. Each mind-set applies to a different area of your game. The first mind-set has to do with your mental attitude while you're playing. The second mind-set has to do with your mental attitude between points. You must apply both of them.

To apply only one and not the other is like trying to climb a ladder that goes only halfway up. You will make it part of the way, but you will not make it to the top. The experienced professional uses both mind-sets to create and maintain the correct environment.

Let me give you an example of how the incorrect mind-sets can affect you on a percentage basis. You played, let's say, three matches in one week. You had many ups and downs during these matches. Your opponent played brilliantly some of

Level 4: Negatives and Positives Applied to Winning

the time. You had bad breaks some of the time. You played terribly some of the time. And you were ahead and lost some of the time. You became upset and lost 20 more points than you normally would have.

You said:

> "If my opponent had not played brilliantly, I could have won."

> "If I was not playing so lousy, I could have won."

> "If I had not gotten all of the bad breaks, I could have won."

> "If I had not missed those easy shots, I could have won."

This kind of thinking is called rationalization. You forgot that "Tennis repeats itself, so lighten up." You easily dropped another 25 points because you play in the "You don't win by trying to win" mind-set and constantly tried to do too much with the ball. (These numbers are conservative. This is over three matches. That's a total of 45 points in a week.)

You played three matches and lost 45 points because you did not use the two mind-sets: "Tennis repeats itself" and "You don't win by trying to win." Multiply 45 times four weeks and we have 180 points a month. Multiply 180 times 12 months and we have a grand total of 2,160 points lost per year.

Can you believe it—2,160 points lost in a year? And that's conservative. Now, to add insult to injury, these points were lost because of your inferior thinking, not because of your opponent's superior playing.

Points are lost because of your inferior thinking, not because of your opponent's superior playing.

The View of Champions

Champions realize adverse situations happen periodically. They are prepared. Instead of letting up, champions stay positive during tough times. They understand that tennis repeats itself. Adverse situations always come and go.

Champions do not get upset or flustered, nor do they lose an extra 20 points a week or an additional 25 points because they play with the "You don't win by trying to win" mind-set. Champions do not lose 2,160 points a year needlessly. Champions realize the seemingly inconspicuous bad decisions a player makes eventually add up and become the difference between winning and losing. The long-term focus champions adopt keep them a notch or two above the competition. They skillfully and effectively neutralize the bad times.

This should be enough to motivate you to learn the correct mind-sets. The disadvantage of losing points because you are not thinking properly should be clear. I must caution you, though. It's not easy to think like this. That's why they call it mental toughness.

It is difficult to remain objective when you're caught up in negatives, mistakes and failures—especially when your emotion takes over. Refocus and evaluate during adverse situations so you can focus on these two mind-sets for the long haul.

Again, those two mind-sets are:

- You do not win by trying to win.
- Tennis repeats itself, so lighten up.

Use these mind-sets the next time you play. Think about the "You do not win by trying to win" mind-set when you attempt to hit too many winners and your unforced errors go up. Then, make the correct mental adjustment.

Level 4: Negatives and Positives Applied to Winning

If you notice things are just not going your way, do not emote, evaluate. Think about the fact that tennis repeats itself. When you feel yourself mentally going off course, pull yourself back in the other direction by remembering these two mind-sets.

Above all, practice, practice, practice. Practice this thinking until you consistently create and maintain an environment that gives your opponent the greatest potential to crack under pressure. Your opponent will not be able to stay with you and will be more prone to make mental and physical errors.

Now that you understand these mind-sets and have a new perspective, you can watch the pros play with an informed eye. The good pros use these concepts all the time. Watch them closely as they rally; they wait patiently for the right opportunity to hit a winner. Watch them closely as they handle their mistakes; they cast them aside and move on. You will be amazed at what you see.

Isolated Situations vs. The Big Picture

What do seasoned professionals know that can help new players? Professionals are skilled at seeing the big picture and applying that knowledge to isolated situations.

Rookies react in a given situation while professionals see the big picture and do not react. They automatically apply what they know to that situation and move on.

This unusual long-term focus in a short-term isolated situation is the main reason professionals create and maintain the correct environment for the long haul.

The emotion of short-term isolated failure does not distract professionals from a long-term focus. The big picture is more real to them than the short-term negatives, mistakes and failures. Professionals learn from experience that this is one of the key elements necessary to win over the competition, who may have equal or more talent.

This book, from beginning to end, is about understanding the same big picture true champions understand. The truth about winning can be viewed through that big picture if you are willing to adopt and use a different way of thinking.

Environmental Stories

Here's a story about Manuel Orantes. It took place at the French Open on slow clay courts. I watched part of the match on television. I say part, because in the opening rounds of a major tennis tournament many matches are played at the same time. The camera moves from court to court, keeping the viewer informed with scores and highlights from the different matches.

At the French Open, the men play three out of five sets to win. Manuel Orantes was losing the match two sets to love. His opponent was up in the third set five games to love and winning the last game 40–love. One more point and the match was over. I didn't think Orantes could win, so I turned off the television and went to bed.

The morning newspaper heralded a victory for Orantes. He won three out of five sets. I was shocked. What turned the match around? Orantes kept creating and maintaining an environment that gave his opponent the greatest potential to crack under pressure.

Orantes was determined to maintain the correct environment until the bitter end, even when he was getting beaten soundly. You never know when the environment you create will give you an opportunity to turn a match around.

It was all over once Orantes got a foothold in the match. That was the most amazing comeback in tennis I have ever seen. (Or should I say, have never seen?)

Orantes worked twice as hard to make this outstanding comeback, because he was playing on a slow clay court. You have to hit many, many more tennis balls on a clay court to win points than on the faster grass or hard court.

You can see why I remembered Orantes and his accomplishment, but cannot remember who his opponent was. (I guess it is just as well for his opponent.)

Here's another example of creating that long-term positive environment. I have never forgotten the great basketball team led by Michael Jordan, the Chicago Bulls of the 90's. Other teams were as good as the Bulls, but could not stay with them for all four quarters.

Michael Jordan and the Bulls had mastered the art of creating and maintaining the correct environment. As I watched them play, I thought: Look at that. The other team is matching them mentally as well as physically.

The problem was the other team could not maintain the correct environment at the level the Bulls were able to maintain it for all four quarters. Eventually, their opponent's level of play dropped, but the Bulls maintained their level and went on to victory.

This is an excellent example of the importance of creating and maintaining an environment that gives your opponent the greatest potential to crack under pressure.

A Different Way of Thinking

You are developing new mind-sets. As with anything else, you have to work at it. Many of the top pros take years to figure this out. Do not assume because they are touring pros that their thinking is correct.

Human nature is human nature whether you are a "C" player or a pro. Creating the correct environment in the face of negatives is difficult for everyone.

It is often the difference between being ranked No. 1 through No. 10 in the world or No. 50 through No. 100. Many pros still think they have to play perfectly or do spectacular things to win when sensible high percentage shots would work.

After reading "The Truth About Winning," you should not fall prey to this thinking.

Review

- You must create and maintain an environment that gives your opponent the greatest potential to crack under pressure.

- To create that environment, you must tilt the odds in your favor by adjusting your thinking in two areas:

  1. You do not win by trying to win.
  2. Tennis repeats itself, so lighten up.

- To apply these two mind-sets correctly, you must master Levels 1, 2 and 3. This gives you the focus necessary to maintain the correct mental environment consistently.

Level 5: The Tennis Warrior

Unexplored Territory

This book is about the correct mental attitude—not your level of play. You can think like a Tennis Warrior at any level. What you learn and apply determines your mental status. Your level of play has nothing to do with it.

The Tennis Warrior mentality is not for everyone, but it can be achieved by anyone willing to take that last mental step.

Plenty of tennis pros have not learned or cannot apply the correct principles you've learned in this book. They live and play on talent and natural ability, which takes them to a certain level, but they never reach the top and stay there.

You must separate the mental from the physical. You can be an intermediate "B" player and still possess exceptional mental abilities. It is completely up to you.

In the first four levels of this book, you learned a way of thinking that affects your ability to play tennis and helps you win more often. Keep applying this information. You will build a strong mental game that improves your physical game.

Practicing your mental game develops mental muscle, just like practicing your physical game develops physical muscle. Practice what you learn and you will be surprised at the mental muscle you develop. Practice what you learn consistently, and the mental strength you need during tough times will be there.

The first four levels establish a high level of thinking and teach you to win a higher percentage of your matches. But, if you'd like to take that extra step into unexplored territory you must grasp the mental dynamics of the Tennis Warrior.

One Step Beyond

The Tennis Warrior understands the big picture (the first four levels) and one dynamic principle that eludes most players—a dynamic principle that can send a player's game into the ozone. This principle is so powerful that tennis pros win with it. Great military leaders focus on it. And successful businessmen and women apply it.

When Tennis Warriors apply this dynamic principle, it carries them one step beyond and leaves the competition in the dust.

Are you curious? You should be. What I am about to tell you has taken most Tennis Warriors years to comprehend and appreciate fully. The dynamic principle that often requires a lifetime to understand is:

Success is based on simple principles.

Surprised? You shouldn't be. This book is all about keeping it simple, advancing from one mental level to the next by learning and practicing simple mental decisions.

These simple mental decisions are the reason you win, and, at this level, you should be determined to make correct mental decisions more often. This mental consistency will catapult your mental game into unexplored territory.

Keen Insight

Tennis Warriors have it all. They understand the big picture (Levels 1 through 4) and they understand the simple nature of winning (Level 5). Tennis Warriors are aware that making the correct decisions and applying the correct solutions is what sets them apart. Tennis Warriors realize the outcome of any event can be determined by a single incorrect or correct thought. Tennis Warriors strive for physical and mental perfection. Tennis Warriors accept that they don't always have control over the physical, but know they have control over the mental.

Tennis Warriors make seemingly insignificant but crucial mental decisions. It's the reason they are good players. Chris Evert, one of the great women tennis champions, summed it up best when she said, "I always knew that I was a good player, but it was when I knew why I was a good player that made all the difference."

Chris was already a great champion. Then, she learned why she was great and started dominating women's tennis. She used and applied the accumulated wisdom from many years of play. This helped her see the big picture and encouraged her to make those subtle decisions that enhanced her ability to create and maintain the correct long-term mental environment consistently.

The reason Chris was great (other than her physical skills) was her ability to make correct mental decisions consistently. She moved up that extra notch into unexplored territory when she captured the importance of making correct decisions.

If this confuses you, let me explain it another way. You may completely understand and be able to apply the first four levels in this book, which can bring you to a very high level of competitive thinking. But, one day, seemingly out of the blue, a light goes on and it clicks. The true importance of making those correct decisions is crystal clear. The big picture comes into focus and you are keenly aware of the impact the correct decision-making process has on the outcome of your matches. You discover how to be a better player, and why you are a better player.

The difference is subtle, but powerful. You are a better player because you realize, for the first time, that winning is truly based on simple principles. And it becomes clear that those simple principles can be controlled by the decisions you make.

Suddenly, thinking correctly becomes top priority, which motivates you even more to make those correct mental decisions that lead to victory.

Tennis Warriors stay with this mental course of applying simple principles even when others do not understand and try to complicate the truth about winning. This is the Tennis Warrior mentality.

A Thinking Paradox

Are you asking: "If these principles are so simple, why do you call it unexplored territory? If these principles are so simple, why isn't everyone a Tennis Warrior?" Unfortunately, an interesting paradox develops when you factor in human nature. Here is the paradox:

The principles that make you successful are simple. That is why it's complicated.

How's that for confusion?

It's complicated because most people refuse to believe it is simple. When something is simple, but you refuse to believe it is simple, it becomes complicated. When you finally become a Tennis Warrior, you realize how simple the principles of winning really are. You also realize most people do not follow them.

Here are three reasons people have trouble believing success is built on simple principles:

1. No one has told them.

2. The outcome of following these simple principles looks complicated. Therefore, they assume the process to achieve that outcome is also complicated. Example: A pro in any sport may display mental toughness and escape from seemingly impossible situations. As you watch, you think: Wow! I cannot believe he was able to do that mentally. The truth is that you saw the result of many years of choosing the simple success principles outlined in this book. The outcome of mental toughness displayed by the pro looks difficult, but the process to achieve that outcome is always based on simple success principles.

3. Following simple success principles consistently requires long-term concentration, the ability to handle failures, and good old-fashioned hard work.

This book is filled with simple mental principles waiting to lift someone up to the mental pinnacle. Will it be you? You can eliminate the first mental roadblock I described above, because I've told you: success is built on simple principles. Now, you must move past the other two. Once you do, you'll be well on your way to becoming a Tennis Warrior.

A Formula for Success

I gave you a formula for success in the Introduction:

Do the simple right. Then, do the simple better.
Then, simply be the best at doing the simple.

Write it down and, when you find yourself mentally going off course, read it. Then, pick up this book and read the section that pertains to your particular situation.

Come back to the simple—always!

Are You Getting It?

The Refocus Technique is difficult to execute, because people become emotionally entangled in their failures, but it really is a simple principle.

The next shot is more important than the last mistake.

Do you know how many people will practice it consistently? Not very many. They are too busy looking for the reason they missed a shot or failed instead of practicing the correct mental attitude.

In contrast, Tennis Warriors are determined to forget negatives, mistakes and failures and move on. They practice forgetting mistakes so much that it is instinctive and automatic. The Tennis Warrior is the best at doing the simple.

On an advanced level, executing simple success principles becomes automatic. This is what Tennis Warriors like Chris Evert discovered. Winning is based on simple principles brought to an advanced level. Do these success principles look familiar?

Acknowledging negatives is not negative thinking.

Mentally tough people think in terms of negatives without being discouraged.

Do not emote. Evaluate.

All negatives are not negative, and all positives are not positive.

You do not win by trying to win.

Tennis repeats itself, so lighten up.

Winning on a professional level is based on these same simple principles executed consistently. Tennis Warriors begin learning how to win with basic principles. Then, when they are on an advanced level, it dawns on them that winning is still based on those same simple principles.

Are you getting it?

The Refocus Technique involves a basic, intermediate and an advanced winning principle. The difference is how automatically you recover from the negatives, mistakes and failures.

Tennis Warriors recover quickly from failures because of all the mental practice. In their minds, failure is part of the process of winning. Remember what Jack Dempsey said? "Success and failure are the same. The only difference is success gets up and keeps going."

As soon as you get up and keep going from your negatives, mistakes and failures, you have made failures part of success. Success and failure are both accepted as part of the journey toward winning in the minds of Tennis Warriors.

Success and failure are the same.

Are they the same to you? This mental attitude is not easy, but you can acquire it if you follow the simple, but powerful, principles in this book—relentlessly.

Are You a Pseudo-Perfectionist?

As a Tennis Warrior, you strive to be a true perfectionist, not a pseudo-perfectionist. What's the difference?

The pseudo-perfectionist is interested only in doing what is physically correct. The true perfectionist is interested in doing what is mentally and physically correct.

Sometimes you see the pros become upset by their negatives, mistakes and failures and cause problems for the judges and linesmen. The commentator usually says the pro acts that way because the pro is a perfectionist and intensely dislikes making mistakes. What do you think?

A perfectionist is someone who desires to do things perfectly, but what is the perfect thing to do when negatives, mistakes and failures occur? Forget them and move on, right?

This is not what the pro did.

A pseudo-perfectionist is interested only in physical, not mental perfection. Part of the definition of perfect is to be complete. Tennis pros who constantly rant and rave about their failures are not complete players. The Tennis Warrior is a true perfectionist and strives to become a complete player mentally and physically.

Characteristics of Tennis Warriors

Tennis Warriors are acutely aware that many physical and mental failures are overcome by taking responsibility for them and adopting the correct mental attitude. Tennis Warriors always choose to learn new mental skills that allow them to adapt quickly without agonizing over past failures or blaming someone else.

Tennis Warriors quickly move away from past failure into the here and now. They are masters of forgetting mistakes and moving on.

This sphere of thinking is the Mental Toughness Sphere. Tennis Warriors are not held hostage by their emotion, which is characterized by subjectivity, over-thinking and dwelling on past failures. Instead, they are tenacious about mentally residing in the Mental Toughness Sphere, which is characterized by objectivity, correct thinking and playing in the here and now.

This single dimensional focus—to reside consistently in the Mental Toughness Sphere—allows Tennis Warriors to develop a multidimensional arsenal of information that can be readily applied to the adverse circumstances of match play.

Tennis Warriors develop this arsenal of information because they are doers. They realize it is not about just knowing the path, but walking the path.

Tennis Warriors apply the solution and move on while most players intellectualize about forgetting their negatives, mistakes and failures. Tennis Warriors realize the ability to apply simple solutions consistently is the mental gateway into the Mental Toughness Sphere and the reason they are a notch above.

Tennis Warriors are aware of the connection between the way they think on the court and the way they think in life. Sports is a microcosm of life, complete with adversity, success, doubt, insecurity, encouragement, discouragement and a plethora of other mental and emotional problems to deal with.

"The Truth about Winning" is a book about thinking, and that thinking can be applied to business, sports or life. If you have not applied the principles in this book to your life, you better read this book again, because you've missed a lot.

You bring your thinking with you wherever you go. Tennis Warriors understand they handle negatives, mistakes and failures in a similar fashion on—and off—the court. Therefore, they strive to improve mental skills and welcome the overflow of these mental skills into their lives.

Champions Think Differently

Put all five levels together and you have the truth about winning—a truth that eludes most people. Most players are too stuck on doing the spectacular or too hung up on their mistakes to ever come close to understanding the truth about winning.

I want you to be different.

I want you to practice these principles on and off the court. I want you to stop being mistake-oriented and start being solution-oriented. I want you to stop looking for excuses and start looking for answers. I want you to stop reacting to isolated situations and start responding to the big picture.

I want you to be a Tennis Warrior. And you can be, because now you know the truth about winning.

Level Summaries

Level 1: Your Perception of Negatives and Positives

To learn how to win, you must learn how to lose correctly.

Acknowledging negatives is not negative thinking. Negative thinking is when you let the negative affect your mental attitude.

Even if you are No. 1 in the world, you will make mistakes. Therefore, it only makes sense to change the way you perceive and are affected by negatives, mistakes and failures.

You must give yourself the freedom to go for your shots, and if you miss, accept it.

This attitude frees you to keep fighting, to keep challenging yourself and to keep taking risks. You do not want your failures or mistakes to be so important in your mind that they stop you from performing. Practicing the correct mental attitude during mistakes and losses is a high priority.

Level Summaries

Level 2: A Technique to Help You Stay Positive

Practice handling your mistakes and failures by using the Refocus Technique:

The next shot is more important than the last mistake.

It keeps you relaxed and objective. Practicing the Refocus Technique consistently trains and conditions your mind to make a quick and automatic mental shift from a negative to a positive without hesitation.

The majority of good pros recover instantly. They have mastered the Refocus Technique so well they no longer separate their negatives, mistakes and failures from their successes or wins.

Remember the Mental Two-Step:

You are always two mental steps away from a positive or negative mental attitude.

The first step, recognizing a negative, is not negative thinking. The second step, deciding if you will let it affect you, is the determining factor.

The choice is yours.

Let the negative affect you and you choose a negative mental attitude. Do not let the negative affect you and you choose a positive mental attitude.

Your thinking must control your emotion rather than your emotion controlling your thinking.

Level 3: Evaluating Negatives and Positives

All negatives are not negative, and all positives are not positive.

Just because something turned out wrong does not mean

your thinking was wrong, and just because something turned out right does not mean your thinking was right. Stop pairing winning with thinking right and losing with thinking wrong. They do not necessarily go together.

Mentally tough people can think negative thoughts without becoming discouraged.

If you haven't learned to deal with negatives and positives correctly, evaluating them properly will be impossible. That is why you must learn Levels 1 and 2 first to understand the truth about winning.

You cannot allow your emotion to control you. You must control your emotion to evaluate properly. This requires practicing the Refocus Technique until your mind automatically relaxes in the face of negatives. Then, and only then, will you be able to evaluate negatives properly.

Do not emote. Evaluate.

Whether you win or lose, you must evaluate with principle, not emotion. You must set your emotions aside. Evaluate on the basis of what really happened, not on what your emotion deceives you into believing happened.

Level 4: Negatives and Positives Applied to Winning

You must create and maintain an environment that gives your opponent the greatest potential to crack under pressure. To do this, you must develop two new mind-sets or ways of thinking.

The first mind-set is:

You do not win by trying to win.

You do not have to do something dynamic, something spectacular or something exciting to win. These are results, not causes. Learn to develop an environment that makes these things happen naturally.

The second mind-set is:

Tennis repeats itself, so lighten up.

You will make mistakes a certain percentage of time whether or not you like it. It's inevitable. Instead of fighting mistakes, master them. Formulate a plan to handle them beforehand.

You must learn to use both of these mind-sets. They help tilt the odds in your favor. Each mind-set applies to a different area of your game. The first mind-set has to do with your mental attitude while you're playing. The second mind-set has to do with your mental attitude between points. You must apply both of them.

Level 5: Unexplored Territory

The Tennis Warrior understands the big picture (the first four levels) and one dynamic principle that eludes most players:

Success is based on simple principles.

The simple mental decisions are the reason you win, and, at this level, you should be determined to make correct mental decisions more often. This mental consistency will catapult your mental game into unexplored territory.

**Do the simple right. Then, do the simple better.
Then, simply be the best at doing the simple.**

The pros do the simple so well that we think it is complicated, but we're confusing the outcome with the process.

Success and failure are the same.

As soon as you get up and keep going from your negatives, mistakes and failures, you have made failures part of success. Success and failure are both accepted as part of the journey toward winning in the minds of Tennis Warriors.

This mental attitude is not easy, but you can acquire it if you follow the simple, but powerful, principles in this book—relentlessly.

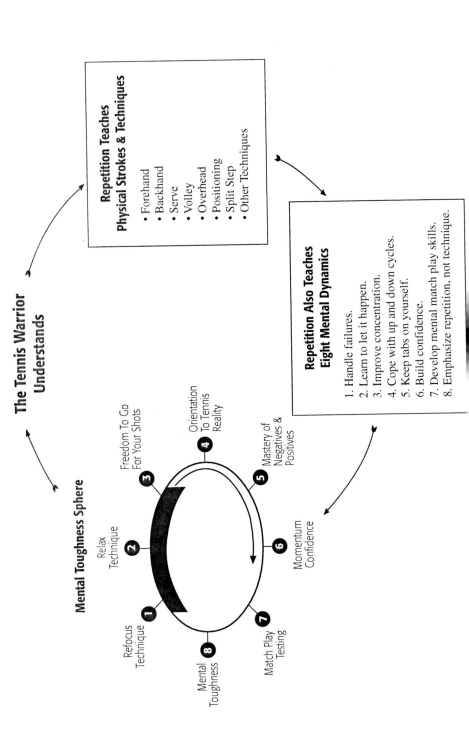

Chart of The Tennis Warrior System

It doesn't matter whether you're a beginner or an advanced player, you can develop mental toughness with the Tennis Warrior System.

The key to learning anything is repetition. Walking, riding a bicycle, driving a car and tieing your shoes are perfect examples. They all require technical skills, but repetition enables you to learn them.

Technical skills are meaningless without repetition.

The Tennis Warrior System emphasizes the repetition of only one or two principles associated with a stroke or technique while you're learning it. This enables you to develop a natural feel for the stroke or technique. You then let the repetition mold you into executing the stroke or technique correctly.

You do not need a lot of technical information. The emphasis is on repetition—not technical skills. (See the "Repetition Teaches Physical Strokes and Techniques" box on the chart.)

As you practice and play, you'll experience failures, successes, tentativeness and anxiety. You also experience physical sensations, such as muscle tightness, relaxation and fatigue. The Tennis Warrior System teaches you how to deal with these. (See the "Repetition Also Teaches Eight Mental Dynamics" box on the chart.)

These mental dynamics create the foundation for the mental skills you need to function inside the Mental Toughness Sphere. You work your way from "Gate 1: The Refocus Technique" to "Gate 8: Mental Toughness" by accumulating and applying correct tennis knowledge incorporated in the sphere.

The principles in the Sphere are proven and time tested. I did not create them. I did, however, harness their power by analyzing, categorizing, labeling and linking them together into one comprehensive, organized system of thinking that enables you to develop mental toughness quickly. You can also tap other sources of knowledge, including coaching, trial and error, books, tapes or a combination of all four.

Your goal is to stay in the Mental Toughness Sphere, where you are not controlled by your emotions.

The chart is an overview of the Tennis Warrior System. It is not intended to be a detailed explanation of it. To learn more about the Tennis Warrior System, please read my books and listen to my audio cassettes.

Please take advantage of my free e-mail tennis lessons. Sign up for them or place your order securely online at www.tenniswarrior.com.

Books and Tapes by Tom Veneziano

Order securely online at www.tenniswarrior.com

Books

The Truth About Winning
Learn the thinking the pros use in a step-by-step fashion.

The Relax Technique
This powerful booklet will help you eliminate anxiety in match play and teach you how to access the correct mental pathway to play in the zone.

Audio Cassettes

The ABC's of Tennis
Learn the nine myths of tennis, the four mental battles you will be up against, the true dynamics of the big "C" (consistency), and much more!

Before-Match Pointers
An excellent cassette to play before your matches. It helps you relax, puts you in the correct frame of mind, and teaches you to go for your shots.

Three Techniques to Increase Your Speed in Tennis
Increase your on-court speed 10 to 40 percent—maybe more! With these three mental techniques, you can increase your speed and you do not have to run sprints or tires to do it. (I know you'll like that part.)

Selecting a Doubles Partner
Learn how to find the correct partner. This cassette addresses the physical and mental skills you and your partner should possess. It will save you a lot of grief.

Think Like a Pro
Save! Purchase the four cassesttes listed above in a convenient album titled, "Think Like a Pro."

About The Author

Tom Veneziano has been an athlete all of his life. He was a wrestler and gymnast in high school, and ventured into the tennis arena his first year of college. Tom began using his Tennis Warrior System from the moment he started playing. With this extraordinary system of thinking incorporated with his playing technique, he quickly attained the No. 1 position on the school tennis team and was granted a tennis scholarship.

Tom graduated in 1971 from Parson's College in Fairfield, Iowa, with a BA degree in Physical Education. His love for tennis inspired him to pursue a career as a teaching pro. Tom works at the Piney Point Racquet Club in Houston, Texas, where he has taught his innovative Tennis Warrior System for over 20 years. Thousands of players have learned to play better tennis, to become mentally tougher, and to win more through this unique system.

Tom writes articles for national magazines and websites, has produced three books and two audio CDs, and writes a monthly online newsletter to help players understand the dynamics of his Tennis Warrior System.